First Ladies

Hillary Rodham Clinton

Joanne Mattern

visit us at
www.abdopublishing.com

Published by ABDO Publishing Company, 8000 West 78th Street, Edina, Minnesota 55439.
Copyright © 2008 by Abdo Consulting Group, Inc. International copyrights reserved in all
countries. No part of this book may be reproduced in any form without written permission from the
publisher. The Checkerboard Library™ is a trademark and logo of ABDO Publishing Company.

Printed in the United States.

Cover Photo: Corbis
Interior Photos: AP Images pp. 16, 31; Corbis pp. 5, 10, 11, 13, 14, 15, 22; Getty Images pp. 6, 8, 9,
   17, 18, 19, 20, 21, 23, 24, 25, 26, 27; Courtesy William J. Clinton Presidential Library p. 7

Series Coordinator: BreAnn Rumsch
Editors: Megan M. Gunderson, BreAnn Rumsch
Art Direction & Cover Design: Neil Klinepier

Library of Congress Cataloging-in-Publication Data

Mattern, Joanne, 1963-
  Hillary Rodham Clinton / Joanne Mattern.
    p. cm. -- (First ladies)
  Includes index.
  ISBN 978-1-59928-792-8
  1. Clinton, Hillary Rodham--Juvenile literature. 2. Presidents' spouses--United States--Biography-
-Juvenile literature. 3. Women legislators--United States--Biography--Juvenile literature. 4.
Legislators--United States--Biography--Juvenile literature. 5. United States. Congress. Senate--
Biography--Juvenile literature. 6. Clinton, Bill, 1946---Juvenile literature. I. Title.

  E887.C55M38 2008
  328.73092--dc22
  [B]

                           2007009729

Contents

Hillary Rodham Clinton

Hillary Rodham Clinton was one of the most exciting First Ladies in U.S. history. Her husband, William J. Clinton, was the forty-second president of the United States. He served as president from 1993 to 2001.

As First Lady, Mrs. Clinton filled many roles. She helped her husband make important decisions. When President Clinton faced personal problems, she stood beside him. Later, Mrs. Clinton began her own political career as a U.S. senator representing New York.

Mrs. Clinton has always been eager to help others. Being First Lady allowed her to do many beneficial things for Americans. Mrs. Clinton has faced challenges of her own, yet she remains an active and powerful woman.

Hillary Rodham Clinton's success has made her a household name in America.

A Strong Start

Hillary Diane Rodham was born in Chicago, Illinois, on October 26, 1947. She was Hugh and Dorothy Rodham's first child. Hugh owned a curtain company, and Dorothy cared for Hillary and her younger brothers. Hugh was born in 1950, and Tony was born in 1954.

Hillary's childhood home was comfortable and spacious. There, she learned to be successful from a young age.

In 1950, the family moved to Park Ridge, Illinois, where Hillary had a happy childhood. She joined Girl Scouts and made friends with many of the neighborhood children. Hillary and her friends played softball and rode their bicycles. Hillary did not care whether she played with boys or girls. She liked playing with everyone!

Hugh and Dorothy were **strict** parents. They expected their children to be well behaved and respectful. Hugh was tough on Hillary and her brothers. Yet, Hillary always knew her father loved her. He encouraged his children to work hard and do their best.

Hillary was just three years old when her family moved to Park Ridge, Illinois.

A Young Leader

In 1961, Hillary entered Maine Township High School East. She studied hard and earned good grades. In her free time, Hillary enjoyed going to sporting events at her school.

Hillary also found time to take part in student council and the **debate** team. She was even elected junior class president! As Hillary became more involved, she realized leadership was fun.

Soon Hillary wanted to be a leader outside of school, too. She did community projects with her church youth group. She and her friends visited children from different Chicago neighborhoods. Hillary also babysat migrant children through one of the church's programs. These experiences

In high school, Hillary's drive to make a difference made her popular among her classmates.

taught Hillary important leadership skills. She learned to reach out to others and try to understand them. Hillary also learned about the different ways people lived. She wanted to make things fair for everyone.

As a senator, Hillary continued speaking about issues she felt were important.

A Clear Path

Hillary transferred to Maine Township High School South for her senior year. She graduated in 1965 and began attending Wellesley College in Massachusetts. Wellesley was one of the country's most renowned all-girls schools. There, Hillary worked hard and became involved in many social issues.

During the 1960s, many students were fighting to make the world better. They wanted equal rights for women and for people of different races. So,

Hillary spoke at her graduation ceremony in 1969. Shortly after, LIFE magazine named Hillary one of the representative student voices of the 1960s.

Hillary's Wellesley professors congratulated her at her graduation ceremony.

they tried to change some unfair laws. Hillary was right in the middle of these activities. She realized that politics could change lives.

In 1969, Hillary was elected student body president at Wellesley. She worked with students and **administrators** to make the school a better place for everyone.

The following autumn, Hillary entered Yale Law School in New Haven, Connecticut. She was one of only 27 women in her class. But, Hillary did not let that stop her. Once again, she became a student leader. It seemed that Hillary preferred to be at the center of the action.

Meeting Bill

In 1970, Hillary met Marian Wright Edelman, a lawyer who worked for children's rights. That summer, Hillary went to Washington, D.C., to assist Edelman with the Washington Research Project. The project was meant to find ways to help migrant families improve their lives. Together, they learned more about the health care and education available to migrant children.

Hillary returned to Yale in the fall. One night in the school library, she saw a young man looking at her. Hillary went over and told him to stop staring and introduce himself. His name was Bill Clinton, and he was from Hot Springs, Arkansas. He was a new student at Yale Law School who wanted to become a politician.

Hillary and Bill had a lot in common. Both of them were interested in politics and public service. And, they both loved to discuss important issues. It didn't take long for Hillary and Bill to fall in love.

In 1973, Hillary graduated from Yale. She began working for the Children's Defense Fund in Cambridge, Massachusetts. Edelman had just started this group, which protected the legal rights of children.

At Yale, Bill and Hillary got to know each other while taking part in mock trials for their law classes.

Working Woman

In 1974, President Richard Nixon was involved in the **Watergate scandal.** Hillary was asked to join the impeachment inquiry staff that was examining evidence against the president. The investigation compelled him to resign.

Meanwhile, Bill had moved home to teach at the University of Arkansas School of Law. Hillary missed Bill very much. So, she moved to Arkansas at the end of summer. She also taught law classes at the university.

Bill soon decided to run for Congress, but he lost the election. Hillary and Bill were married the following year on October 11, 1975. Then, they went right back to work. Bill's second election was successful. In 1976, he became **attorney general** of Arkansas.

Hillary and Bill were married in their living room. The couple was happy they could finally start their life together.

Hillary's knowledge of law made her a valuable member of the impeachment inquiry staff.

Investigating a President

Impeachment is the process of conducting a trial to remove a public official from office. In the United States, impeachment has rarely been used against a president. In 1868, Andrew Johnson became the first president to be impeached. In 1974, Richard Nixon became the second president in U.S. history to face impeachment.

President Nixon was suspected of covering up a break-in at the Watergate complex in Washington, D.C. Nixon hoped to acquire private information that might help him win reelection.

In January 1974, Hillary joined a committee of lawyers working to determine if President Nixon should be impeached. The committee members read reports, listened to taped telephone conversations, and studied the U.S. Constitution. On July 19, the committee reported its findings to the U.S. House of Representatives. The report clearly outlined the reasons why Nixon should be impeached.

On August 5, the public was informed about a tape called the "smoking gun." It proved Nixon was involved in an illegal cover-up. President Nixon did not want to face his impeachment trial. So, he resigned from office on August 9.

The **attorney general**'s wife was not expected to have a career. But, Hillary worked as a lawyer with the Rose Law Firm. Hillary also started a group called Arkansas Advocates for Children and Families. This group provided legal help for poor families.

Changing Roles

In 1978, Mr. Clinton ran for governor of Arkansas. He was still **attorney general**, so Mrs. Clinton helped him with the campaign. When her husband won the election, Mrs. Clinton became the First Lady of Arkansas. Governor Clinton asked his wife to lead a state government health care program to help people from rural areas. She happily contributed, while also working at the Rose Law Firm.

There had never been a First Lady in Arkansas who worked full-time and had a government job, too! So, many people were not used to the way Mrs. Clinton approached her new role. She even kept her maiden name. But, the First Lady did not pay attention to people's doubts. Instead, she kept working hard at what she loved.

Mrs. Clinton loves being a mother. She has often said she would have liked to have had more children.

The Clintons also wanted to have a family. They soon welcomed a daughter on February 27, 1980. The proud parents named the baby Chelsea after a song they liked.

In 1980, Mr. Clinton's reelection campaign was unsuccessful. However, in 1982 he ran again and won. This time, he asked his wife to run a committee to change Arkansas's school system. Again, people worried about the First Lady's involvement. But, Mrs. Clinton did her best work and ignored the complaints.

Mrs. Clinton was very busy helping her husband with his campaign. She spoke to many people and learned about their needs. She was a strong support for Mr. Clinton.

A New Image

The Clintons celebrated their election victory with Al Gore, the new vice president, and his wife, Tipper.

Governor Clinton was very popular. But he and Mrs. Clinton wanted to do more for the country. So, he decided to run for president of the United States. Mr. Clinton won the election! So in 1993, Mrs. Clinton became America's First Lady. She was eager to share her ideas with her husband and work as a team.

Not everyone was happy with Mrs. Clinton's involvement. Some people complained that they had elected Bill Clinton, not his wife. The First Lady tried to explain that she had chosen a career. She said she was not the kind of woman who stayed home

Mrs. Clinton enjoyed touring several Asian countries with her daughter. While in India, they visited the Taj Mahal.

and baked cookies. But this upset many Americans, and Mrs. Clinton realized she sounded too harsh.

So, the First Lady worked hard to change her image. Her looks had never mattered much to her before. But now, she styled her hair and wore nicer clothes. She was more careful about what she said, too. Mrs. Clinton did not mind making these small changes to help her husband's career.

The Clintons also worried about their 12-year-old daughter, Chelsea. They wanted her to have a normal childhood. So, they tried to keep Chelsea's picture out of newspapers. They also made sure she had fun. Chelsea often had friends sleep over at the White House. And, she traveled around the world with her parents.

Big Lessons

The Clintons were eager to help America. Soon after his election, President Clinton asked his wife to lead a committee to change national health care laws. Mrs. Clinton spent many months traveling around the United States. She spoke with doctors, lawyers, and patients to gather information. Then, she held meetings and wrote reports.

The First Lady felt strongly about improving health care. She wanted to help the people she had spoken with.

Finally in September 1993, the First Lady presented her report to Congress. She asked for several big changes to the health care system. But, Congress did not agree with the First Lady's ideas. Some people felt she was pushy and had too much power. So, her changes were never made.

Mrs. Clinton was angry and disappointed. But she learned two important lessons. She discovered that small steps work better for making big changes. And, she realized teamwork is an important part of solving a problem.

The Clintons also learned about honesty. In 1994, they were accused of being involved in the Whitewater **scandal**. Fortunately, they were able to prove their innocence. This helped President Clinton win reelection in 1996.

Whitewater

In the 1970s, the Clintons purchased a piece of property along the White River in Arkansas. The property was to become a set of vacation homes called Whitewater Estates. They planned to later sell the property to make money. Unfortunately, no one wanted to buy the property. Investors lost money on the deal and became angry. They accused the Clintons of knowing about the money problems.

Then in 1993, the Clintons learned their partner, Jim McDougal, was using their money illegally. Lawyers and other officials questioned the Clintons to find out if they knew about McDougal's plan. Mr. and Mrs. Clinton were innocent. But, they did not want everyone to know about their private lives. Because they were secretive, many Americans thought they were guilty.

A lawyer named Kenneth Starr continued the investigation for many months. Eventually, it cost more than $70 million. But no evidence was ever found that proved the Clintons had done anything wrong.

On the Campaign Trail

In 1998, President Clinton went to court for another **lawsuit**. Even though he promised to tell the truth, President Clinton committed a serious crime called **perjury**. Because he lied, the House of Representatives voted to **impeach** him. But in February 1999, the Senate decided President Clinton was not guilty. Even though the First Lady was angry that her husband had lied, she stayed beside him.

President Clinton was nearing the end of his second term as president in 2001. Now, many people thought Mrs. Clinton should run for office. In 2000, Senator Daniel Patrick Moynihan of New York was ready to retire. Mrs. Clinton decided to run for his seat.

The First Lady was relieved when the Senate decided President Clinton was not guilty during his impeachment trial. Now the Clintons could go back to their normal lives.

Mrs. Clinton knew a lot about politics, but she had not yet run for public office herself. She faced many new challenges. And, she learned a lot about running her own campaign.

In order to be a senator in New York, Mrs. Clinton needed to live there. So, the Clintons bought a house near New York City. However, Mrs. Clinton was not home much. She spent many months traveling around the state to meet New Yorkers and give speeches. She called this trip a "listening tour."

Mrs. Clinton worked hard on her campaign. The New Yorkers she met inspired her to win the race and represent them in Congress.

Senator Clinton

On November 7, 2000, Mrs. Clinton became the only First Lady elected to public office. Now, she was Senator Hillary Rodham Clinton!

Senator Clinton was one of only eleven women elected to the Senate in 2000. Soon, she was appointed to serve on three Senate

Senator Clinton's family supported her as Al Gore conducted the oath of office.

Senator Clinton worked with former New York City mayor Rudolph Giuliani to help New York recover after September 11. Senator Clinton was proud when President George W. Bush agreed with her plan.

committees. Senator Clinton used her position to bring jobs and other kinds of help to New York communities. She also worked on children's health and education causes.

On September 11, 2001, a **terrorist** attack destroyed the World Trade Center in New York City. Senator Clinton knew that New York would need a lot of help from the federal government. People near the area required medical care, and companies needed money to stay in business.

Senator Clinton was determined to help New York recover from the tragedy. She persuaded the U.S. government to give $21 billion to the city. The money was used to help New York clean up and rebuild.

A Bright Future

Senator Clinton remained active in other parts of her life as well. In 2001, she and Mr. Clinton proudly watched Chelsea graduate from college and begin a new career in New York City. And in 2003, the senator wrote a book about her life called *Living History*.

When Mr. Clinton suddenly got sick in September 2004, Senator Clinton rushed to be at his side. He had an operation on his heart, and she helped him through his recovery. At the same time, Senator Clinton continued her work in Congress and was reelected in November 2006.

Throughout her life, Hillary Rodham Clinton has worked hard to improve the lives of many Americans. Today, she

Senator Clinton's book was a big success. She previously wrote a book called It Takes a Village: And Other Lessons Children Teach Us.

is one of the most powerful women in politics. In fact, she made history in early 2007 when she announced she would run for president in 2008. Many people wonder if Hillary Rodham Clinton will become America's first female president. The world will be watching to see what the future holds for this dynamic woman.

The Clintons enjoyed a moment together at the opening of the William J. Clinton Presidential Library and Museum on November 18, 2004.

Timeline

1947	Hillary Diane Rodham was born on October 26.
1961–1965	Hillary attended Maine Township high schools East and South.
1965–1969	Hillary attended Wellesley College.
1973	Hillary graduated from Yale Law School; Hillary worked for the Children's Defense Fund.
1974	Hillary investigated the Watergate scandal.
1975	Hillary married Bill Clinton on October 11.
1976	Mr. Clinton was elected attorney general of Arkansas; Mrs. Clinton joined the Rose Law Firm; Mrs. Clinton founded Arkansas Advocates for Children and Families.
1978	Mr. Clinton was elected governor of Arkansas.
1980	The Clintons' only child, Chelsea, was born on February 27.
1982	Mr. Clinton was reelected governor of Arkansas.
1993–2001	Mrs. Clinton acted as America's First Lady, while Mr. Clinton served as president.
2000	Mrs. Clinton was elected senator of New York.
2001	Mrs. Clinton raised funds to help New York after September 11.
2003	Mrs. Clinton wrote *Living History*.
2006	Mrs. Clinton was reelected senator of New York.

Did You Know?

Mrs. Clinton was the first president's wife to keep her maiden name, Rodham.

The Clintons named their daughter Chelsea after the song "Chelsea Morning" by Joni Mitchell.

Mrs. Clinton was the only First Lady to keep an office in the West Wing. She and her staff called it Hillaryland.

As First Lady, Mrs. Clinton wrote a weekly newspaper column called "Talking it Over."

Mrs. Clinton once served as the honorary president of the Girl Scouts of America.

Former First Lady Eleanor Roosevelt is one of Mrs. Clinton's biggest role models.

On October 8, 2005, Senator Clinton was inducted into the National Women's Hall of Fame.

Mrs. Clinton is the first female senator to represent New York State.

Glossary

administrator - a person who manages an operation, a department, or an office.

attorney general - the chief law officer of a national or state government.

debate - a discussion or an argument.

impeach - to charge a public official with misconduct in office.

lawsuit - a case held before a court.

perjury - telling a lie when under oath to tell the truth.

scandal - an action that shocks people and disgraces those connected with it.

strict - demanding others to follow rules or regulations in a rigid, exact manner.

terrorist - a person who uses violence to threaten people or governments.

Watergate - a 1972 political crime involving President Richard Nixon. Nixon's aides broke into the Watergate complex to steal campaign information about his opponent. The burglars were caught and sent to jail. Nixon resigned in 1974.

Web Sites

To learn more about Hillary Rodham Clinton, visit ABDO Publishing Company on the World Wide Web at **www.abdopublishing.com**. Web sites about Hillary Rodham Clinton are featured on our Book Links page. These links are routinely monitored and updated to provide the most current information available.

Index